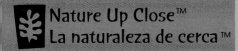

Nature Up Close™
La naturaleza de cerca™

Bees Up Close
Las abejas

Katie Franks
Traducción al español:
Ma. Pilar Sanz

PowerKiDS press™ & **Editorial Buenas Letras**™
New York

Published in 2008 by The Rosen Publishing Group, Inc.
29 East 21st Street, New York, NY 10010

First Edition

Editor: Jennifer Way
Book Design: Kate Laczynski
Photo Researcher: Nicole Pristash

Photo Credits: Cover, pp. 1, 5, 7, 9 (inset) 11, 13, 15, 17, 19, 21, 24 © Studio Stalio; p. 9 (main) © Shutterstock.com; p. 23 by Alessandro Bartolozzi.

Cataloging Data

Franks, Katie.
    Bees up close–Las abejas / Katie Franks; traducción al español: Ma. Pilar Sanz. — 1st ed.
        p. cm. — (Nature up close–La naturaleza de cerca)
    Includes index.
    ISBN 978-1-4042-7676-5 (library binding)
    1. Honeybee—Juvenile literature. 2. Spanish language materials I. Title.

Manufactured in the United States of America

Websites: Due to the changing nature of Internet links, PowerKids Press and Editorial Buenas Letras have developed an online list of Web sites related to the subject of this book. This site is updated regularly. Please use this link to access the list: www.powerkidslinks.com/nuc/bee/

Contents

Contenido

This is a honeybee. Bees are known for making honey.

Esta es una abeja. Las abejas hacen miel.

5

A bee has many body parts. Some of these are the **stinger**, the **antennae**, the wings, and the legs.

El cuerpo de una abeja tiene diferentes partes. Algunas partes son el **aguijón**, la **antena**, las alas y las patas.

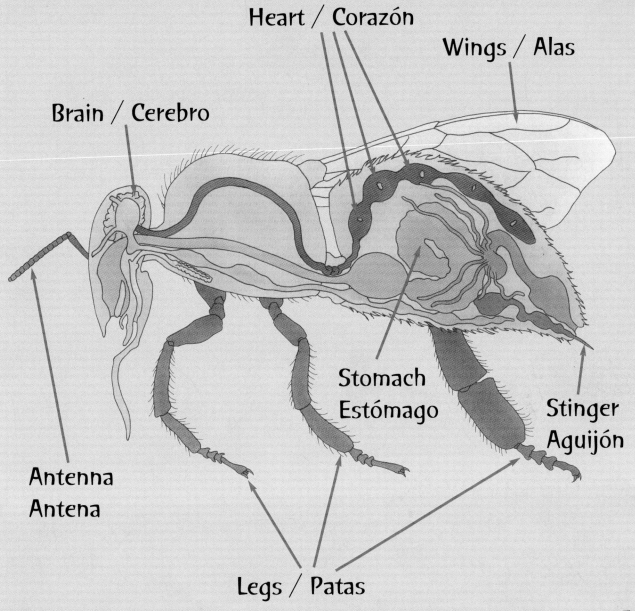

Heart / Corazón

Wings / Alas

Brain / Cerebro

Stomach
Estómago

Stinger
Aguijón

Antenna
Antena

Legs / Patas

7

Bees have a special mouthpart called a **proboscis**. The proboscis is used to help bees eat.

Las abejas tienen una parte especial en la boca llamada **probóscide**. La probóscide ayuda a las abejas a comer.

Proboscis / Probóscide

Bees live in a **hive** in a group called a **colony**. The colony has worker bees, drones, and a queen. The queen leads the colony.

Las abejas viven en **colmenas**, en grupos llamados **colonias**. Las colonias tienen abejas obreras, zánganos y una abeja reina. La abeja reina es la líder de la colonia.

Queen / Reina

Worker / Obrera

Drone / Zángano

Worker bees gather nectar and pollen to bring back to the hive. Nectar and pollen are found in flowers.

Las abejas obreras colectan néctar y polen, y lo llevan a la colmena. El néctar y el polen se encuentran en las flores.

Worker bees build the hive using a wax that is made by their body. Hives are made up of honeycombs.

Las abejas obreras construyen la colmena con cera que crece en sus cuerpos. Las colmenas están formadas por panales.

Honeycombs can hold honey, bee eggs, or growing bees. In these drawings, you can see how an egg grows into an adult bee.

Los panales pueden almacenar miel, huevos de abeja y abejas adultas. En estos dibujos puedes ver cómo crece un huevo hasta ser una abeja adulta.

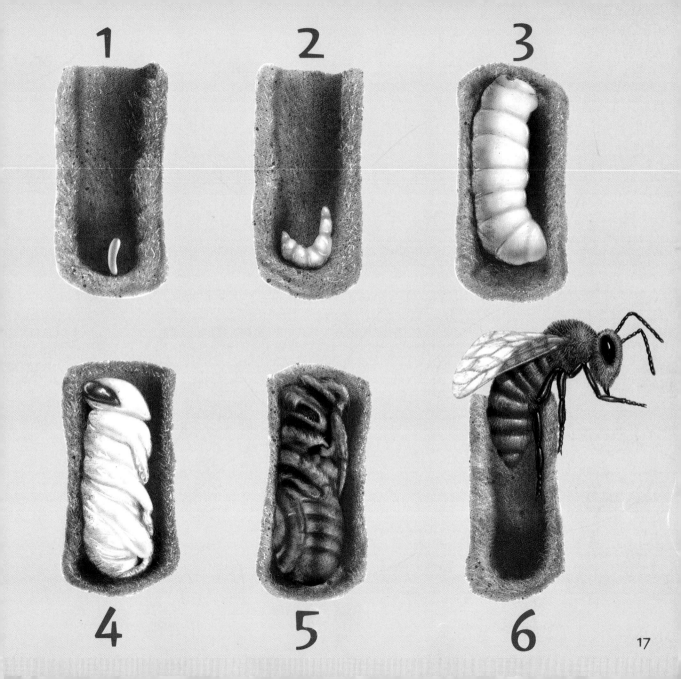

1   2   3

4   5   6

When the colony gets full, the queen and some of the bees leave to start a new colony.

Cuando se llena la colonia, la reina y algunas otras abejas se van a formar una nueva colonia.

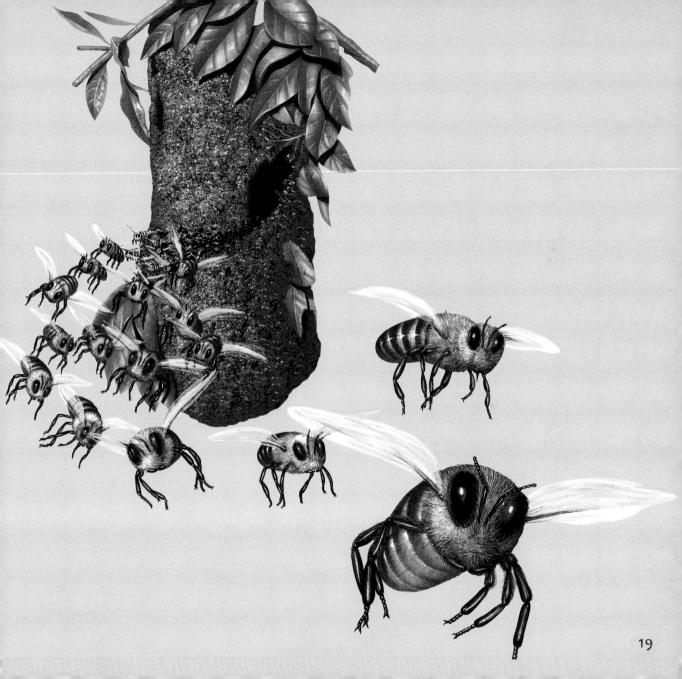

Beeswax can be made into **candles**. Honey is used as food.

La cera de las abejas se usa para fabricar **velas**. La miel se usa para comer.

Bees live all around the world. On this map of the world, the places where bees live are shown in brown.

Las abejas viven en todo el mundo. En este mapa puedes ver, en color marrón, los lugares en los que viven las abejas.

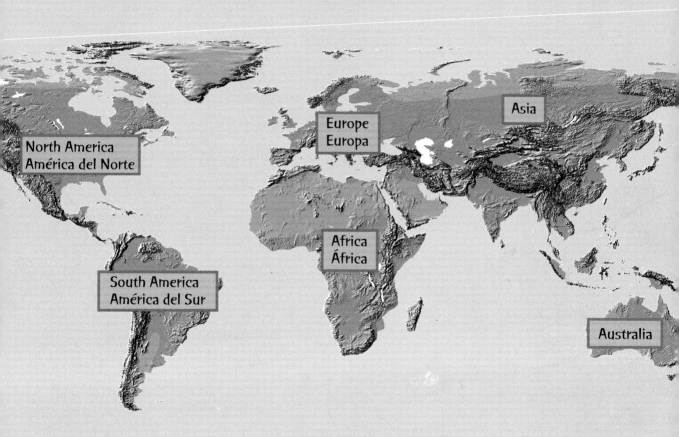

North America
América del Norte

Europe
Europa

Asia

South America
América del Sur

Africa
África

Australia

23

Words to Know / Palabras que debes saber

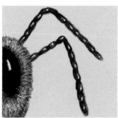

antennae
(las) antenas

candles
(las) velas

colony
(la) colonia

hive
(la) colmena

proboscis
(la) probóscide

stinger
(el) aguijón